To

_____

From

_____

the fruit *of the* SPIRIT
Bible study for tweens

CAMELLIA
HOUSE PUBLISHING

T.S. Dobson

the fruit of the SPIRIT

a Bible Study for Preteens

Copyright 2014 by Teresa Scott Dobson

ISBN—13: 978-1500641658
ISBN—10: 1500641650

All Scripture quotations in this book are taken from the King James Version, New International Version, and New Living Translation.

Cover art by Teresa Scott Dobson

Editor: Matthew Dobson (author of the Living With Purpose series)

We hope you enjoy this book. Our goal is to provide direction on the Fruits of the Holy Spirit. To give Biblical guidance on how to look up the fruits using the Bible and apply to everyday living. Different versions of the Bible are at the user's discretion. We would like to recommend that a Bible with a Concordance be used with this Bible study.

CAMELLIA
HOUSE PUBLISHING

Camellia House Publishing, Century, FL

Printed in the United States of America.

the fruit *of the* SPIRIT   T.S. Dobson

CONTENTS

Acknowledgements

With special thanks:

To my children,

Hillary, Abby, Anna Marie, and David, for filling my life with unconditional love and joy.

To my husband,

Matthew, for his prayer and guidance as a positive thinker, Christian leader, and his constant love and support throughout my career.

To my extended family,

Through all the experiences in life, insight given, the sum of all this gave me knowledge to reach for my future.

To my friends,

Memories and life lessons taught through your friendship and kindness.

To God,

Without you nothing is possible, and with you ALL THINGS ARE POSSIBLE through your love. You teach us to live by the fruits of the HOLY SPIRIT.

Galatians 5:22-23 (NIV)

22 But the fruit of the Spirit is love, joy, peace, patience, kindness, goodness, faithfulness, 23 gentleness and self-control. Against such things there is no law.

Introduction

When I started this journey with the Fruits of the Spirit, I was drawing a tree on the black chalkboard wall in the Youth Sunday School room. After redesigning the room for the kids I started drawing the tree and began thinking about the Fruits of the Spirit. It seemed that God was trying to tell me to teach the next few weeks about this topic. So from there I wrote the Fruits of the Spirit around the tree. With only simple notes on paper, I came up with a way to teach kids how to read the Bible using the concordance with the topic of the Fruits. This was the first time the kids had ever used the concordance of their Bible. At this point, I knew it was time to start training them about the usefulness of the concordance and felt it would be a good study to share with others.

At the tween age, or preteen age, kids need to understand how to start interpreting the Bible, comprehending the terms of the Bible.

As an artist, illustrator, and teacher, God continues to use me. He wanted me to put a study together to help kids better understand key terms such as the Fruits of the Spirit to teach them how important these are to their lives. By having these nine important fruits, this will help them grow in the knowledge of Christ; grow in the knowledge of what God, Christ, and the Holy Spirit mean.

These studies are not limited to just tween age children. They can be used with any age, but the target is to start increasing children's knowledge at early ages. This book is a good gift for anyone, or a good study to use in your church Bible-study classes. My hope is that the study will help the adolescent child practice the fruits of the Holy Spirit in their daily lives.

God bless!

Definition of LOVE

Function: *noun* 1 : a quality or feeling of strong or constant affection for and dedication to another <motherly *love*> 2 the strong affection and tenderness felt by someone **b** : a beloved person **3 a** : warm attachment, enthusiasm, or devotion **b** : the object of attachment or devotion **4** : **in love** : feeling love for and devotion toward someone

God gives us unconditional love. Let us learn the fruit of the Spirit of Love, and what the Bible has to say about it.

the fruit of the SPIRIT T.S. Dobson

We learn about many types of love growing up. There's tough love, love of family, love of friends, puppy love, and even love of material things.

"Tough love!" I've heard that once or twice growing up.

As children, at some point in our lives we've experienced tough love from a parent or adult. You may not have been told what tough love is. But through the experience you have gained some insight on it. So what is tough love?

I'll give an illustration of something that happened between me and my daughter Abby. Abby had just turned ten years old and had made a list of things she desired for her birthday. One of those things on her list was written in larger print than the rest; meaning this was the one thing she wanted the most. She had many items that weren't so costly, but then there's always the large gift. To make a long story short, she didn't get the big gift for two reasons. One it was costly and two, at her age it didn't seem to be a necessity, but a want. After the party, we discussed why she didn't get all she wanted and reluctantly she understood.

Sometimes we get what we need rather than what we want, and in the end it's better for us. Sometimes we don't always know the difference between wants and needs, but God does, and so do most parents. There will be times in our lives, that we get what we want, but we must know that it's not usually free, and sometimes comes with a cost.

There are many other types of love out there. There's the love of parents, grandparents, sisters and brothers, relatives, and friends. There's the love of a spouse, like moms and dads have for one another. We also learn by other's love how to give love in return. You show love to your grandparents by holding their hand and listening to old stories they tell you. This can show a love and respect towards them.

the fruit of the SPIRIT   T.S. Dobson

The love of your mom, dad, grandparents, family members, and friends are very important to have growing up. It's important to know you have security in your family and friends through all stages of life. It's good to know that love is there.

"Ewe, puppy love?" Puppy love is better known as feelings of love or infatuation, often felt by young people during their childhood. It's named for its resemblance to the affection that may be felt for a puppy. But if you've ever had a "crush" on someone and it didn't work out, love can turn to some other feeling or emotion like anger or sadness.

Like birthday items you wish for: computer, phone, and the list goes on and on; these are all material things. Yes, as we get older we find a need for a phone to contact family and friends to let them know how we are doing. You can use phones for important dates, and we use them in emergency situations. We find a need for a computer when it involves communication and work. We find many needs for these items sooner or later, but even in the midst of these needs or wants, they are all material. So what does material mean? It can mean the need we have for clothes, or the want of toys. Material things cost money. So that pretty much sums it up! There's lots of material things on this earth. Sometimes we develop a love for many material things in our lives. Material love effects us all in some ways, but how we manage this love can effect our lives big and small.

As you can see, love varies depending on what kind it is. The illustrations about love relates to the Bible. It relates not only as the Fruit of the Spirit, but God's love for us. Let's take a look at the next page and see why God showed the ultimate love for us. These different types of love and what God has to say about them.

the fruit of the SPIRIT T.S. Dobson

What the Bible has to say about LOVE

You won't find it in the dictionary under the definition of love, but God's love trumps all the love there is on this earth. God loves all of his creation.

In the Bible John chapter 3 verse 16 (John 3:16) says, "For God so loved the world, that he gave his only begotten Son, that whosoever believeth in him should not perish, but have everlasting life."

God showed us the ultimate love, by sacrificing his one and only Son that we might all have life and have it more abundantly. This means he loves you and me very much! His love has no bounds. God's love is unconditional, meaning without limitations; like the love of your parents. No matter how many times you might disagree or disappoint, parents love you. God's love never ends, even after this life on earth, his love is Eternal. We are special creations of God.

In 1 John 4:7-12 God explains His Love and how we are to love others: "Dear friends, let us love one another, for love comes from God. Everyone who loves has been born of God and knows God. Whoever does not love does not know God, because God is love. This is how God showed his love among us: He sent his one and only Son into the world that we might live through him. This is love: not that we loved God, but that he loved us and sent his Son as an atoning sacrifice for our sins. Dear friends, since God so loved us, we also ought to love one another. No one has ever seen God; but if we love one anther, God lives in us and his love is made in us."

In Exodus 20:12 it says, "Honor thy father and thy mother; that thy days may be long upon the land which the LORD thy God giveth thee." By honoring your parents with love and respect you will live a happy life here on this earth. With that honor comes praise from them and a glorious praise rewarded by God.

What does God have to say about material love? In Matthew 6:19-20 it says, "Lay not up for yourselves treasures upon earth, where moth and rust doth corrupt, and where thieves break through and steal: But lay up for yourselves treasures in heaven, where neither moth nor rust doth corrupt, and where thieves do not break through nor steal." So what does this mean? Although it's not bad to have material things, we need to remember the most important thing in life doesn't have to do with earthly material things. Coming to know Christ, who He is, and what he did on the cross for us gives us hope for an eternal life, this is far better than anything of material value on earth. As you can see God wants us to experience love in many different ways on earth. He wants us to give love to others as we get love in return. We are to be Christ like and love one another.

the fruit of the SPIRIT   T.S. Dobson

Concordance Study Time:

Using a Bible with a Concordance in the back, find at least 5 verses about LOVE. Write them down below. Write the Book and verse number only. This will be a quick reference for you on the Fruit of Love. Then go to those verses in the Bible and study those verses.

_____

_____

_____

_____

_____

Read the verses you jotted down above, then come up with our own version of what those verses mean to you. Break down at least one of the verses you chose about LOVE. If you don't understand a term in the verse, look it up in the dictionary so that you can relate to what the Bible is saying to you.

_____

_____

_____

_____

_____

_____

(This page may be reproduced to use in a bible study group.)

the fruit *of the* SPIRIT   T.S. Dobson

Question & Answer Response:

1. What did you learn about the fruit of the spirit of LOVE?

_____

_____

_____

2. How can you use this fruit in your own life?

_____

_____

_____

_____

3. Can you name an experience in your life where you didn't show the spirit of love or feel the spirit of love?

_____

_____

_____

_____

_____

Prayer Time:

Lord, thank you for teaching me about the Spirit of Love. Lord I want to serve you by showing others that I possess the spirit of Love. Like a lighthouse, help me to be a light of Love towards others. Forgive me for where I have failed You in this Spirit and bring me closer to you Oh Lord. I ask these things in Jesus name. Amen.

(This page may be reproduced to use in a bible study group.)

Definition of JOY

Function: *noun* 1: a feeling of great happiness

2: a source or cause of great happiness : something or someone that gives joy to someone

3: success in doing, finding, or getting something

God wants us to show the spirit of joy to others. Let us learn the fruit of the Spirit of Joy, and what the Bible has to say about it.

the fruit *of the* SPIRIT T.S. Dobson

Joy! In other words, delight or happiness. Something good or desired.

Have you ever experienced the joy of having a little brother or sister be born, or maybe even a baby cousin? It's a wonderful feeling isn't it?

We've all experienced some type of joy in our lives. Whether it is a present you've been wanting for a long time, or as simple as going swimming on a hot summer afternoon with friends; joy can come from many circumstances surrounding us. Sometimes you might find joy in playing sports, finally understanding a tough math question, or better yet, making a good grade on a test. But what do all there joys have in common?

The answer is that they come and go. One minute there's joy your younger baby sister or brother gives, but then as they get older sometimes disagreements happen. Your joy can be up and down. Sometimes those nice swims on a hot summer afternoon start with joy and end with sadness in the pouring rain. Our sense of what joy is can change.

But maybe you should look at joy differently. It doesn't have to be fleeting. It can be constant. Don't you want to feel joyful all the time? Why of course! We all do!

Let's look now at what our Lord has to say about joy. Let's get into the Bible and see.

What the Bible has to say about JOY

Let's look in the Bible at John 17:13. Jesus said, "I am coming to you now, but I say these things while I am still in the world, so that they may have the full measure of my joy within them."

Jesus prayed that the disciples would have joy. He also wants us to have joy in our lives.

A favorite song, for many people is "Joy to the World." The words speak for themselves. "Joy to the world, the Lord is come! Let earth receive her King; Let every heart prepare Him room, And heaven and nature sing, And heaven and nature sing, And heaven, and heaven, and nature sing." That's the first line of the song. This means Jesus came to the earth, and if we open our hearts and receive him, we will have joy, not just a worldly joy, but a heavenly joy. This is what the song is about.

Christians aren't meant to walk around with a sad look on their face. If we truly understand what it means to be saved, we know that God loves us. That was the first fruit we discussed. By knowing you have His love, you can experience the second fruit of joy. This is a complete joy, not one of temporary feelings. It's a permanent joy that can only be found in God. God's son Jesus paid the price for us to have eternal joy.

The apostle James said, "Consider it all joy...when you encounter various trials, knowing that the testing of your faith produces endurance" (James 1:2-3). There will be times when you don't feel joyful; after a math test you didn't do so well on, but you stay strong in the faith, and try to do better next time. If you seek joy during hard times in you life and joy will come back. Keep your focus on God our heavenly Father to keep your joy constant. Joy comes from knowing we are never alone.

God's joy is everlasting! That is why it is considered one of the Fruits of the Spirit.

Concordance Study Time:

Using a Bible with a Concordance in the back, find at least 5 verses about JOY. Write them down below. Write the Book and verse number only. This will be a quick reference for you on the Fruit of Joy. Then go to those verses in the Bible and study those verses.

_____

_____

_____

_____

_____

Read the verses you jotted down above, then come up with our own version of what those verses mean to you. Break down at least one of the verses you chose about JOY. If you don't understand a term in the verse look it up in the dictionary so that you can relate to what the Bible is saying to you.

_____

_____

_____

_____

_____

_____

(This page may be reproduced to use in a bible study group.)

the fruit of the SPIRIT   T.S. Dobson

Question & Answer Response:

1. What did you learn about the fruit of the spirit of JOY?

_____

_____

_____

2. How can you use this fruit in your own life?

_____

_____

_____

_____   _____

3. Can you name an experience in your life where you didn't show or feel the spirit of joy?

_____

_____

_____

_____

_____

Prayer Time:

Lord, thank you for teaching me about the Spirit of Joy. Lord I want to serve you by showing others that I have the spirit of Joy. Like a lighthouse, help me to be a light of Joy towards others. Forgive me for where I have failed You in this Spirit and bring me closer to you Oh Lord. I ask these things in Jesus name. Amen.

(This page may be reproduced to use in a bible study group.)

PEACE

3

Definition of PEACE

Function: *noun* **1** a state of tranquility or quiet

2: freedom from civil disturbance

3: a feeling of security or order within a community provided for by law or custom

4: harmony, freedom from hostility, content

God wants us to have peace in our daily living. Let us learn the fruit of the Spirit of Peace, and what the Bible has to say about it.

the fruit of the SPIRIT   T.S. Dobson

"Peace!"

I'm sure you've heard that a time or two. Many people say it loud and proud and using their hands they make the peace sign. Peace symbols are used on clothes and other apparel.

But what do they mean?

Sometimes people refer to the peace sign because they are happy and feel free.

Many times we refer to peace when we see wars and fights breaking out around the world. You might not understand why people can't just get along with each other. Some things we will never understand. It can be discouraging to turn on the news and see all the negative out there.

What about that small argument you had with your mom, dad, brother or sister? You have to learn to compromise, or meet in the middle so to speak, to truly feel contentment and peace after an argument. Sometimes we struggle to understand close friends. Having peace in relationships is important, but what's more important is inner peace within. At times we struggle with peace, and life doesn't always seem fair. But if we have inner peace, that will overflow into peace towards others.

We all want to have a peace that lasts. Wouldn't it be nice if we turned the television on, and all we heard was positive news about peace around the world?

Peace in the world only lasts for a short while as we have seen. War will never end on earth (until the peaceful reign of Christ) no matter how hard people try.

Believe it! There is an everlasting peace you can have. Do you want a lasting inner peace?

Let's look now at what our Lord has to say about peace. Let's get into the Bible and see.

the fruit *of the* SPIRIT   T.S. Dobson

What the Bible has to say about PEACE

John 14:27 says, "Peace I leave with you; my peace I give you. I do not give to you as the world gives. Do not let your hearts be troubled and do not be afraid."

Jesus spoke of peace in John 14:27 the eve before he was crucified. Even in this time before his death, Jesus wanted us to experience peace on this earth. He wanted to leave us with peace. He wanted us to have this and place it close to our hearts. In the wars of trouble throughout the Bible, Jesus was named the "Prince of Peace" (Isaiah 9:6) says, "For to us a child is born, to us a son is given, and the government will be on his shoulders. And he will be called Wonderful Counselor, Mighty God, Everlasting Father, Prince of Peace." And even now in the times of trouble on this earth, we must know that the Lord still wants this for us all.

True peace is the work of the Holy Spirit in our lives!

There is another symbol far more important than the peace symbol we so often see. It's the symbol of the cross that represents a bridge of peace that is not of this earth but of Heaven. The cross was the bridge that closed the gap between us and Heaven. Jesus died on a cross to open up the Heavens to save us all from the wars of this earth, so that we might experience true peace that can only come from God.

When you are going through worry, fear, or just a busy day, you should remember who your God is. Trust in Him, and you will experience His peace that surpasses all understanding.

Once we have accepted Jesus as our Savior; once we have repented of our sins and are faithful to Him in Christian living; we discover a peace with God.

Now a lasting thought from the Bible on peace comes from 2 Thessalonians 3:16, "Now may the Lord of peace himself give you peace at all times in every way."

the fruit of the SPIRIT   T.S. Dobson

Concordance Study Time:

Using a Bible with a Concordance in the back, find at least 5 verses about PEACE. Write them down below. Write the Book and verse number only. This will be a quick reference for you on the Fruit of Peace. Then go to those verses in the Bible and study those verses.

_____

_____

_____

_____

_____

Read the verses you jotted down above, then come up with our own version of what those verses mean to you. Break down at least one of the verses you chose about PEACE. If you don't understand a term in the verse look it up in the dictionary so that you can relate to what the Bible is saying to you.

_____

_____

_____

_____

_____

_____

(This page may be reproduced to use in a bible study group.)

the fruit *of the* SPIRIT   T.S. Dobson

Question & Answer Response:

1. What did you learn about the fruit of the spirit of PEACE?

_____

_____

_____

2. How can you use this fruit in your own life?

_____

_____

_____

_____

3. Can you name an experience in your life where you didn't show or feel the spirit of peace?

_____

_____

_____

_____

Prayer Time:

Lord, thank you for teaching me about the Spirit of Peace. Lord I want to serve you by showing others that I have the spirit of peace. Like a lighthouse, help me to be a light of peace towards others. Forgive me for where I have failed You in this Spirit and bring me closer to you Oh Lord. I ask these things in Jesus name. Amen.

(This page may be reproduced to use in a bible study group.)

PATICENCE

4

Definition of PATIENCE also known as long-suffering

Function: *noun* **1** the capacity or fact of being patient

2: to endure hardship without complaint

3: tolerant and even-tempered

4: quiet or steady perseverance

God wants us to learn how to be patient. Let us learn the fruit of the Spirit of Patience, and what the Bible has to say about it.

the fruit of the SPIRIT   T.S. Dobson

"Are we there yet?" "Are we there yet?"

"Be patient! Be patient!" Parents seem to say that the most!

It takes patience for many things in our lives; like that long trip to a fun and exciting vacation. The excitement builds mile after mile until we get closer and closer to our destination. Patience can be hard to find!

What about your gifts under the Christmas tree? They sit there for days wrapped up with a pretty bow on top. You get curious and impatient...so you walk up to the tree and look around to make sure no one is looking. Then you quietly sneak up to the gift and pick it up. You shake it to see what it might be. You can't seem to figure out what's inside. You put it down and get a little frustrated at knowing you have ten more days to wait and see what it is. It takes patience, so you roll your eyes and walk away.

You practice patience when a baby brother, sister, or cousin keeps asking you silly questions. It even takes patience to get your teeth cleaned in the dentist chair.

"Chores?" Yes, chores. How do chores teach us anything about patience?

Sometimes chores help us to be patient. If we do chores we can earn money and good things. As you may have heard before, "patience pays off!" A week of chores washing dishes, throwing out the trash, and cleaning your room requires patience. But if you do them on a daily basis, it can make you feel good that you accomplished something.

Practice makes perfect! That's been said in the name of sports many times. The more practice we do at something the better we get. It takes patience to become better at whatever we are trying to accomplish. Whether it's sports or even learning a new musical instrument it takes time.

There are many times when we need to use the fruit of patience on long vacation trips, holidays, family situations, and everyday chores.

Let's look at what the Bible has to say about patience.

the fruit *of the* SPIRIT   T.S. Dobson

What the Bible has to say about PATIENCE

Hebrews 6:15 says, "And so, after he had patiently endured, he obtained the promise." In James 1:3 it says, "Knowing this, that the trying of your faith worketh patience."

These verses describe what it's like to wait for a promised vacation. We see ourselves on earth taking a trip of a lifetime. There are new destinations to visit on earth, but the ultimate trip awaits us—one where the skies are always clear, the flowers are always blooming, and the water is always calm. Heaven isn't that far away and it's the perfect vacation that awaits us. God not only wants us to learn patience when going on a simple trip, but also in our journey to our final destination of Heaven. Heaven will be eternal life.

Romans 8:25 says, "But if we look forward to something we don't yet have, we must wait patiently and confidently."

We are like the Christmas gift that you cannot see and have tried to be patient in opening. Jesus knocks on our hearts to see what's inside. He remains patient for us to open our hearts and let him come inside. When we open a present under the tree we embrace it and hold it dear to us. Jesus wants to be part of our lives. We must see him as a gift that God has given.

Revelation 2:19 states, "I know all the things you do. I have seen your love, your faith, your service, and your patient endurance. And I can see your constant improvement in all these things."

Like doing chores, God looks at our works. Meaning our spiritual works, what we do on earth for His glory, will pay off in the end. If we live for the Lord and use the spirit of patience no matter what the circumstance, we are practicing the fruit of the Holy Spirit.

Patience

GOOD things are going to HAPPEN

the fruit *of the* SPIRIT   T.S. Dobson

Concordance Study Time:

Using a Bible with a Concordance in the back, find at least 5 verses about PATIENCE. Write them down below. Write the Book and verse number only. This will be a quick reference for you on the Fruit of Patience. Then go to those verses in the Bible and study those verses.

_____

_____

_____

_____

_____

Read the verses you jotted down above, then come up with our own version of what those verses mean to you. Break down at least one of the verses you chose about PATIENCE. If you don't understand a term in the verse look it up in the dictionary so that you can relate to what the Bible is saying to you.

_____

_____

_____

_____

_____

_____

_____

(This page may be reproduced to use in a bible study group.)

the fruit *of the* SPIRIT   T.S. Dobson

Question & Answer Response:

1. What did you learn about the fruit of the spirit of PATIENCE?

_____

_____

_____

2. How can you use this fruit in your own life?

_____

_____

_____

_____

3. Can you name an experience in your life where you didn't show or feel the spirit of patience?

_____

_____

_____

_____

_____

Prayer Time:

Lord, thank you for teaching me about the Spirit of Patience. Lord I want to serve you by showing others that I have the spirit of Patience. Like a lighthouse, help me to be a light of Patience towards others. Forgive me for where I have failed You in this Spirit and bring me closer to you Oh Lord. I ask these things in Jesus name. Amen.

(This page may be reproduced to use in a bible study group.)

KINDNESS

Definition of KINDNESS

Function: *noun* **1** the state of quality of being kind

2: a kind act

3: nice behavior or friendly feeling

4: considerate or helpful act

God wants us to show kindness to others. Let us learn the fruit of the Spirit of Kindness, and what the Bible has to say about it.

the fruit *of the* SPIRIT   T.S. Dobson

"ONE ACT OF KINDNESS CAN HEAL A THOU-
SAND HURTS." While walking down the street in
Asheville, North Carolina I saw these words on a sign
that a man was holding. I thought about it all day and
what it meant.

We should be willing to give and receive kindness from
others.

Willing to give kindness to others—what does that
mean? It means a friendly hello to someone you normal-
ly don't talk to at school or in town; not talking bad
about someone in front of others; picking up someone's
trash when they drop it on the floor; opening a door for
someone; sweeping the floor even when it's not expected
of you; giving a few cents to someone in need. These are
all ways to show kindness to others.

Willing to receive kindness from others. What does this
mean? Sometimes people do things for us and we take it
for granted. A simple "thank you" goes a long way.
When getting gifts, clothes, and food; all these things deserve thanks. If we show our appreciation—that's being
kind. What about that outfit that you got for Christmas
you thought wasn't so pretty? Instead of acting upset
because it wasn't the outfit you wanted, we should be
grateful and show kindness toward the person who gave
us the gift. Our reaction with gratitude shows how we
can receive things with kindness.

There are times that friends or even family can be un-deserving of your kindness. But remember to take the high road. This means be the bigger person, and still show kindness. This can help heal in a situation. You might not get a "pat on the back" for taking the high road in conflict with someone, but eventually your act of kindness will not go unnoticed by others. Show mercy towards them. Try putting yourself in somcone else's shoes. What would it feel like to be them? By thinking this way, we can see if we showed kindness in the right way.

The Golden Rule holds true meaning for the fruit of kindness. What is the Golden Rule? Let's see what God has to say about the Golden Rule and kindness.

the fruit *of the* SPIRIT   T.S. Dobson

What the Bible has to say about KINDNESS

God explains to us what the Golden Rule means in the Bible.

Luke 6:31 says, "Do unto others as you would have them do to you."

The Golden Rule is simple. Let us always try to do good toward all people—those in our lives that we are close to and even those that are strangers. We should try to show kindness regardless of what clothes they wear, how they smell, and even with their not so nice attitudes.

Many times before getting to know them we judge someone based on what they wear or how they act. Sometimes we speak terrible things about someone we heard without knowing the whole truth of the matter. The Golden Rule states we should treat someone the way we want to be treated. Putting yourself in someone else's shoes helps us to see if what we might have said wasn't kind. If someone tells you something about another person and you didn't hear it from that person, it's best not to repeat it.

I'm sure there have been times you were guilty of not acting in a kind way. After all, we are human, and we have all been guilty of this a time or two. But the good news is that God gives us second chances. He shows us kindness by giving us another chance. This is just like our parents or loved ones who give us second chances when we do wrong. This is an act of mercy and kindness. God wants us to show the fruit of kindness towards others.

Practice kindness like Jesus did. Forgive grudges from friends, don't talk about others, help someone in need, and give a smile to show kindness.

Luke 6:38 says, "Give, and it will be given to you..." Give kindness towards others, and get kindness in return. This can be said about all the fruits of the Holy Spirit we are learning.

If we truly want to be closer to God we must act Christ-like with a spirit of kindness. Jesus spoke of God's kindness in the Sermon on the Mount. "But I say to you, love your enemies, bless those who curse you, do good to those who hate you, and pray for those who spitefully use you..." This doesn't sound like it would be easy to do; at times it's not. God shows us kindness by loving us; we our His children.

Create Kindness

 T.S. Dobson

Concordance Study Time:

Using a Bible with a Concordance in the back, find at least 5 verses about KINDNESS. Write them down below. Write the Book and verse number only. This will be a quick reference for you on the Fruit of Kindness. Then go to those verses in the Bible and study those verses.

_____

_____

_____

_____

_____

Read the verses you jotted down above, then come up with our own version of what those verses mean to you. Break down at least one of the verses you chose about KINDNESS. If you don't understand a term in the verse look it up in the dictionary so that you can relate to what the Bible is saying to you.

_____

_____

_____

_____

_____

_____

_____

_____

(This page may be reproduced to use in a bible study group.)

 *the* fruit *of the* SPIRIT T.S. Dobson

Question & Answer Response:

1. What did you learn about the fruit of the spirit of KINDNESS?

_____

_____

_____

2. How can you use this fruit in your own life?

_____

_____

_____

_____

3. Can you name an experience in your life where you didn't show or feel the spirit of kindness?

_____

_____

_____

_____

_____

Prayer Time:

Lord, thank you for teaching me about the Spirit of Kindness. Lord I want to serve you by showing others that I have the spirit of Kindness. Like a lighthouse, help me to be a light of Kindness towards others. Forgive me for where I have failed You in this Spirit and bring me closer to you Oh Lord. I ask these things in Jesus name. Amen.

(This page may be reproduced to use in a bible study group.)

GOODNESS

6

Definition of GOODNESS

Function: *noun* 1 the state or quality of being good

2: moral excellence, virtue

3: a kind feeling; generosity

4: worthiness, being worthy

God wants us to show goodness to others. Let us learn the fruit of the Spirit of Goodness, and what the Bible has to say about it.

the fruit *of the* SPIRIT T.S. Dobson

Have you ever said the words, "Goodness gracious!" Why do we say that? Maybe you said it because you were surprised, excited, or shocked by something. Did you realize that you are asking God's grace of goodness when you speak it. Sometimes we say things without knowing their true meaning. Our use of words take on a different meaning at times. Goodness is what makes people like you and love you. The way you show goodness can help you gain friends. Like the fruit of kindness from the last chapter, being good is an act of being kind; they go together.

Right vs. wrong? We try to do what's good, but there are times you might not always do good. If you find yourself doing bad, learn from your mistakes and strive to do better.

At times when you do good your parents tend to reward you. For example, we make a good grade on our report card and you get rewarded for studying.

There are times when you do good for others, but aren't rewarded by material things. For example, you take food to a person who is in need. You might get gratitude or thanks in return. The feeling of joy that you helped someone in need is a reward in itself. This is a way to experience the real fruits of the spirit. You can begin feeling joy and peace for your acts of goodness towards others. This is a lasting feeling that trumps or is greater than any material reward we might get. Goodness is just that, being good.

It's never too late to do goodness in your life. Each day is a new day to show goodness.

Let's take a look in the Bible and see instances and times where God showed kindness and how we are to use the Fruit of Goodness in our lives.

the fruit *of the* SPIRIT   T.S. Dobson

What the Bible has to say about GOODNESS

In Luke 6:45 it says, "A good man brings good things out of the good stored up in his heart, and an evil man brings evil things out of the evil stored up in his heart. For the mouth speaks what the heart is full of."

Another important verse in the Bible about goodness is Galatians 6:9-10 where it says, "Let us not become weary in doing good, for at the proper time we will reap a harvest if we do not give up. Therefore, as we have opportunity, let us do good to all people, especially to those who belong to the family of believers." Don't give up on doing good for others, no matter who they are, or what they have done. God doesn't give up on us in our time of need, therefore we shouldn't give up on others. Step up and ask adults what you can do to help someone in your community. You might have a friend or an acquaintance at school who needs to see the good you can give. Show goodness by asking someone if they need help. You can always pray to God to help you discern or know who is in need of your goodness and mercy.

When you show goodness God is proud you are one of His children because you are showing the fruits of the Holy Spirit. You are becoming closer to God. When you do this you are being Christ-like in your actions, which makes you a son or daughter of our Lord.

In Psalm 23:6, it states, "Surely goodness and mercy will follow me all the days of my life, and I will dwell in the house of the LORD forever." God makes this promise for us because of His Love and Goodness. He wants us to experience His goodness. He will not forget the good you do here on earth.

Like the song verse, "Surely goodness and mercy shall follow me, follow me all my days, all the days of my life." Let God's goodness overflow in your life.

Search for ways and pray to have this fruit of Goodness from the Holy Spirit.

GOODNESS

the fruit of the SPIRIT   T.S. Dobson

Concordance Study Time:

Using a Bible with a Concordance in the back, find at least 5 verses about GOODNESS. Write them down below. Write the Book and verse number only. This will be a quick reference for you on the Fruit of Goodness. Then go to those verses in the Bible and study those verses.

_____

_____

_____

_____

_____

Read the verses you jotted down above, then come up with our own version of what those verses mean to you. Break down at least one of the verses you chose about GOODNESS. If you don't understand a term in the verse look it up in the dictionary so that you can relate to what the Bible is saying to you.

_____

_____

_____

_____

_____

_____

_____

(This page may be reproduced to use in a bible study group.)

the fruit *of the* SPIRIT   T.S. Dobson

Question & Answer Response:

1. What did you learn about the fruit of the spirit of GOODNESS?

_____

_____

_____

2. How can you use this fruit in your own life?

_____

_____

_____

_____

3. Can you name an experience in your life where you didn't show or feel the spirit of goodness?

_____

_____

_____

_____

Prayer Time:

Lord, thank you for teaching me about the Spirit of Goodness. Lord I want to serve you by showing others that I have the spirit of Goodness. Like a lighthouse, help me to be a light of Goodness towards others. Forgive me for where I have failed You in this Spirit and bring me closer to you Oh Lord. I ask these things in Jesus name. Amen.

(This page may be reproduced to use in a bible study group.)

FAITHFULNESS

7

Definition of FAITHFULNESS

Function: *noun* **1** the quality of being faithful

2: true to one's word, promises, vows

3: steady in affection; loyalty

4: consistent with truth and trust

God wants us to show faithfulness to others. Let us learn the fruit of the Spirit of Faithfulness, and what the Bible has to say about it.

the fruit *of the* SPIRIT   T.S. Dobson

"Have a little faith!" You might have heard that line when your parents try and convince you things are going to be alright. When your sitting in the dentist chair, you can be sure the dentist knows best how to fill a cavity. Use a little faith and belief he or she knows what they are doing when they work on your teeth. If you have a pain in your tooth and you want relief, the only way to experience relief is to trust that filling the cavity is going to help make it better. First you put trust and faith in your parents to get you to the dentist, and second put trust in your dentist to fix the problem.

Sometimes it only takes a little faith to go a long ways.

Faith is important in many areas of our lives. Having faithfulness in a friend is one area. A faithful friend is a loyal friend. A friend that is steadfast, means they stay in your life through good and bad, through ups and downs, and through disagreements. This is a true friend and shows faithfulness in friendship.

You may not realize it, but you can have faith in filling your belly with food when you are hungry. We have faith that our family will provide us food daily. Faithfulness in our family's love for us, is a security in affection.

Sometimes we have faith in material things. For example, you want to wake up at a specific time in the morning so you use an alarm clock to wake you up. You put your faith in a clock that can get you up on time for school. What happens when the electricity goes out during the night? The clocks alarm doesn't go off and you might wake up late. The faith in that alarm clock quickly diminishes. Faith in material things are short lived.

When a person makes a promise to you and they don't keep it, then faith in that person becomes weak. Maybe you didn't keep a promise—it's not the end; you can still strive to be more faithful. Ask forgiveness when you fall in your faith.

What does true Faithfulness mean? What does God have to say about faithfulness and how you should live by faith on earth? Let's take a look.

the fruit *of the* SPIRIT   T.S. Dobson

What the Bible has to say about FAITHFULNESS

In Matthew 17:20 Jesus said, "Because you have so lit-tle faith. Truly I tell you, if you have faith as small as a mustard seed, you can say to this mountain, "Move from here to there,' and it will move. Nothing will be impos-sible for you."

Jesus said to His disciples in Luke 17: 5-6 "The apostles said to the Lord, "Increase our faith! The Lord replied, 'If you had faith the size of a mustard seed, you could say to this mulberry tree, 'Be uprooted and planted in the sea,' and it would obey you.'"

Why a mustard seed? A mustard seed is very tiny but once it grows it can provide food for animals. Our faith may start out small, but once it grows it becomes stronger and can change our lives.

As the saying goes F.R.O.G. "First Rely on God." You must put your faith in God and rely on him. Don't be worried or afraid of what you can and cannot do. When you have troubles in your life or need guidance you should pray to God. Have faith in God that he will help you make the right decisions. Rely on God even when you have to go to the dentist. Pray that He will guide the dentist or doctors hands. Put your faith in Him first!

You must place your dependence on God. The ultimate in faithfulness comes from being willing to do God's work in your life. If you do this you can accomplish great things.

In 1 John 1:9 it says, "If we confess our sins, he is faithful and just and will forgive us our sins and purify us from all unrighteousness."

If you are dealing with hurt from a friend, or something you did that hurt someone else, pray to God that he will help heal that friendship. Put you're faith in Him. If you allow the Lord to come into your heart, he will forgive you of your sins. He is faithful in forgiving us as Christians when we fail. Remember God will always be loyal to you.

Show the fruit of faithfulness even as small as a mustard seed and it will continue to grow into more than the faith we put in this world. A Heavenly Faith awaits us!

faithfulness

 *the* fruit *of the* SPIRIT   T.S. Dobson

Concordance Study Time:

Using a Bible with a Concordance in the back, find at least 5 verses about FAITHFULNESS. Write them down below. Write the Book and verse number only. This will be a quick reference for you on the Fruit of Faithfulness. Then go to those verses in the Bible and study those verses.

_____

_____

_____

_____

_____

Read the verses you jotted down above, then come up with our own version of what those verses mean to you. Break down at least one of the verses you chose about FAITHFULNESS. If you don't understand a term in the verse look it up in the dictionary so that you can relate to what the Bible is saying to you.

_____

_____

_____

_____

_____

_____

_____

(This page may be reproduced to use in a bible study group.)

the fruit *of the* SPIRIT   T.S. Dobson

Question & Answer Response:

1. What did you learn about the fruit of the spirit of FAITHFULNESS?

_____

_____

_____

2. How can you use this fruit in your own life?

_____

_____

_____

_____

3. Can you name an experience in your life where you didn't show or feel the spirit of faithfulness?

_____

_____

_____

_____

_____

Prayer Time:

Lord, thank you for teaching me about the Spirit of Faithfulness. Lord I want to serve you by showing others that I have the spirit of Faithfulness. Like a lighthouse, help me to be a light of Faithfulness towards others. Forgive me for where I have failed You in this Spirit and bring me closer to you Oh Lord. I ask these things in Jesus name. Amen.

(This page may be reproduced to use in a bible study group.)

GENTLENESS

Definition of GENTLENESS also known as meekness

Function: *noun* **1** the capacity or fact of being gentle

2: not severe

3: mildness of manners or disposition

4: not hard or forceful

God wants us to show gentleness to others. Let us learn the fruit of the Spirit of Gentleness, and what the Bible has to say about it.

"Be real gentle!" is common phrase you might hear. "Gentle" is a word that represents many things in life. You might have been told to be gentle picking up a baby animal for the first time or holding a baby brother or sister. "Be gentle!" When holding an egg.

"Be gentle with your words" is another phrase. This means be careful with what you say. Sometimes words hurt others and choosing to be gentle means not being harsh or getting angry with your actions. A gentle reaction tends to produce more friends, and less enemies. As we learned about of the fruit of kindness, those that have an attitude of kindness tend to treat others with gentleness. Don't be so quick to anger.

Gentleness can be seen in the elderly. Older people tend to have more of a gentle spirit because of their experiences. Their age teaches them patience and not to be rash.

Gentleness is controlled strength!

It takes a strong person to be gentle, not a weak person. Why? Because a strong person must carefully watch what they say in a situation so that they know the right words and not say something to upset someone. It takes a strong person to turn the other cheek when someone offends them. If someone says something to hurt your feelings try not to react harshly. Try to say something positive. For instance, your friend says to you, "I don't like your shoes." You could respond harshly and say, "Well I don't care what you think." Or you might reply,

"Everyone is entitled to their own opinion," and leave it at that. Take the high road with gentleness. Next time they may not be so quick to judge what you wear and your gentleness may rub off on them. Show tolerance when needed towards them. This can change others hearts.

Like holding an egg gently, we must treat others gently by knowing the right things to do and say.

How do we know how to treat others with gentleness?

Let's look at what the Bible has to say about how we are to use the Fruit of the Spirit of Gentleness.

the fruit *of the* SPIRIT   T.S. Dobson

What the Bible has to say about GENTLENESS

Philippians 4:5 says, "Let your gentleness be evident to all."

God desires us to be kind and loving. When using gentleness, people will feel loved by you. When people feel loved by you they will see Jesus in you. Always strive to be humble and kind; this will show your gentleness.

What does even-tempered mean? It means to not be harsh or get so easily annoyed by something. For instance, if a friend said something rude to you it takes a strong person to react with calmness. It's hard for most to do, but true Godly gentleness is required.

In 2 Timothy 2:25-26 it says, "Opponents must be gently instructed, in the hope that God will grant them repentance leading them to a knowledge of the truth, and that they will come to their senses and escape from the trap of the devil, who has taken them captive to do his will."

The devil likes to see hostility towards others. Christians should try and act strong in gentleness toward others when offended. Try to say the right things and don't fuel more anger from a person. By doing this they will want to find out why you are being nice and gentle to them. Like God shows us gentleness when we don't deserve it, we need to spread gentleness towards others. Make it contagious!

Do you need more of the spirit of gentleness? The answer to that is we all do! We all must want to be less quick to judge and more open to a gentle spirit. Nothing is won by force.

Titus 3:2 explains, "to speak evil of no one, to avoid quarreling, to be gentle, and to show perfect courtesy toward all people."

Ask God to help show you how to be gentle towards others. Ask him to help you know what to say in tough situations.

Concordance Study Time:

Using a Bible with a Concordance in the back, find at least 5 verses about GENTLENESS. Write them down below. Write the Book and verse number only. This will be a quick reference for you on the Fruit of Gentleness. Then go to those verses in the Bible and study those verses.

_____

_____

_____

_____

_____

Read the verses you jotted down above, then come up with our own version of what those verses mean to you. Break down at least one of the verses you chose about GENTLENESS. If you don't understand a term in the verse look it up in the dictionary so that you can relate to what the Bible is saying to you.

_____

_____

_____

_____

_____

_____

_____

(This page may be reproduced to use in a bible study group.)

the fruit *of the* SPIRIT   T.S. Dobson

Question & Answer Response:

1. What did you learn about the fruit of the spirit of GENTLENESS?

_____

_____

_____

2. How can you use this fruit in your own life?

_____

_____

_____

_____

3. Can you name an experience in your life where you didn't show or feel the spirit of gentleness?

_____

_____

_____

_____

Prayer Time:

Lord, thank you for teaching me about the Spirit of Gentleness. Lord I want to serve you by showing others that I have the spirit of Gentleness. Like a lighthouse, help me to be a light of Gentleness towards others. Forgive me for where I have failed You in this Spirit and bring me closer to you Oh Lord. I ask these things in Jesus name. Amen.

(This page may be reproduced to use in a bible study group.)

SELF CONTROL

Definition of SELF CONTROL also known as restraint

Function: *noun* **1** the ability to control one-self or one's actions, feelings

2: controlling behavior

3: controlling impulses

God wants us to show self control to others. Let us learn the fruit of the Spirit of Self Control, and what the Bible has to say about it.

the fruit *of the* SPIRIT   T.S. Dobson

Self control or controlling yourself is not the easiest thing to do.

Having self control is required to function in society. You see something you want in the shop through the front window. You might have plenty of leftover birthday money to buy it but it would take all of your money to get it. So you practice self control to keep you from buying it right away. Sometimes we buy things on impulse, or in other words do something too quickly. Then after we buy it we see it somewhere else cheaper. Our desires and wants must have some sort of control on them or we can get out of control in spending the money we've saved.

The same can be said about decisions we make day to day. Decisions can impact our lives both positively and negatively. So you must practice self control in order to keep you moving in the right direction.

Use self control when talking about others. Try not to say bad things about people, and try not to judge them. Learn to hold your tongue and not speak.

Self control is needed in many areas of your life, not just with money. How about when someone makes you mad? Your first reaction might be to yell at them or fight. But you must take a deep breath and think about the consequences of your actions. If you were to get into a fight you might face punishment. Lack of self control can cause bad things to happen to you.

One of the most difficult fruits of the spirit is self control because it's part of a decision making process that impacts you; self control with money, relationships, eating habits, and sports. Don't rely too much on material things.

Material things? Yes, sometimes material things can get in the way of healthy relationships with your family and friends. Spending too much time playing a game on your phone or television can cause you to lose sight of other important things like hanging out with friends; reading a book that you need to read before class tomorrow; and participating in daily exercise. Self control is needed so you can tell yourself to only spend a certain amount of time on these things daily so you don't miss out on life. So how do we know how to use this thing called self control?

Let's look at the ninth Fruit of the Holy Spirit of Self Control.

the fruit *of the* SPIRIT   T.S. Dobson

What the Bible has to say about SELF CONTROL

Proverbs 21:23 says, "He who guards his mouth and his tongue, Guards his soul from troubles." Watching what we say about others can keep us from troubles.

Proverbs 29:11, "A fool always loses his temper, But a wise man holds it back." Be slow to anger, by using self control.

In 1 Corinthians 9:24-27 Paul speaks about self control and self discipline while running a race.

"24 Do you not know that in a race all the runners run, but only one gets the prize? Run in such a way as to get the prize. 25 Everyone who competes in the games goes into strict training. They do it to get a crown that will not last, but we do it to get a crown that will last forever. 26 Therefore I do not run like someone running aimlessly; I do not fight like a boxer beating the air. 27 No, I strike a blow to my body and make it my slave so that after I have preached to others, I myself will not be disqualified for the prize."

What does this mean? Paul is comparing this race to our life on earth. If you have ever played sports and ran in a race you would know it takes discipline to work hard at it and compete. To finish the race when it's really hard and you don't think your body can do it; it takes discipline and self control. In the end you get a prize if you do well.

Our lives can be compared to a race. The race for eternal life lasts more than our time on earth. The greatest of all races leads to eternal life. Everyone can be a winner. With God you don't have to compete with another person. He loves you. He wants you to finish on earth with self control and discipline. Live a good life here so you can say you gave it your all. There will be times when you make mistakes, but that is part of being human. God wants you to continue to apply this fruit to your lives even when you have failed. Pick yourself up and dust yourself off and finish the race.

Simply put, self control is learning to say yes to what is right, and no to what is wrong. God wants you to pray when making decisions, even if it's a quick decision you should say a quick prayer to find out what is needed.

Concordance Study Time:

Using a Bible with a Concordance in the back, find at least 5 verses about SELF CONTROL. Write them down below. Write the Book and verse number only. This will be a quick reference for you on the Fruit of Self Control. Then go to those verses in the Bible and study those verses.

_____

_____

_____

_____

_____

Read the verses you jotted down above, then come up with our own version of what those verses mean to you. Break down at least one of the verses you chose about SELF CONTROL. If you don't understand a term in the verse look it up in the dictionary so that you can relate to what the Bible is saying to you.

_____

_____

_____

_____

_____

_____

_____

(This page may be reproduced to use in a bible study group.)

the fruit *of the* SPIRIT   T.S. Dobson

Question & Answer Response:

1. What did you learn about the fruit of the spirit of SELF CONTROL?

_____

_____

_____

2. How can you use this fruit in your own life?

_____

_____

_____

_____

3. Can you name an experience in your life where you didn't show or feel the spirit of self control?

_____

_____

_____

_____

Prayer Time:

Lord, thank you for teaching me about the Spirit of Self Control. Lord I want to serve you by showing others that I have the spirit of Self Control. Help me to have Self Control in my life. Forgive me for where I have failed You in this Spirit and bring me closer to you Oh Lord. I ask these things in Jesus name. Amen.

(This page may be reproduced to use in a bible study group.)

But the fruit of the spirit is

LOVE JOY
PEACE
PATIENCE
KINDNESS
GOODNESS
FAITHFULNESS
GENTLENESS
SELFCONTROL

against such things there is no law.

Galatians 5:22-23

Plan of Salvation

To have the Fruits of the Holy Spirit applied to your life you must know what God has done for you. To truly receive everlasting love, joy, peace, patience, kindness, goodness, faithfulness, gentleness, and self control in your life you must understand how much He loves you.

In John 3:16 it says, "For God loved the world so much, that He gave his one and only son so that everyone that believes in him will not perish, but have Eternal life."

How can I be saved? The steps to salvation are as easy as **A.B.C.**

ADMIT—Admit that you are a sinner in need of God.

BELIEVE—That Jesus died and rose again for your sins.

CONFESS—That Jesus Christ is Lord of your life.

"Whoever calls on the name of the Lord shall be saved." Romans 10:13

Your salvation experience is the beginning of your personal relationship with Jesus Christ.

You must now say the sinners prayer:

Lord Jesus,

I know I am sinner and need your forgiveness. I know you died on the cross for me. I now turn from my sins and ask you to forgive me. I now invite you into my heart and life. I now trust you as Savior and follow you as Lord. Thank you for saving me. Amen.

Scripture promises if you have accepted Christ:

1 John 5:11-13
And the witness is this, that God has given us eternal life, and this life is in His Son. 12He who has the Son has the life; he who does not have the Son of God does not have the life. 13These things I have written to you who believe in the name of the Son of God, in order that you may know that you have eternal life.

If you have prayed the above prayer or one like it for the first time please let us know so we can rejoice with you and pray for you. Email: teresadobson1@aol.com. If you have a church family let them know of your decision. If you don't have a church find one close to you to worship the Lord and fellowship with other believers.

Diary Notes:

Diary Notes:

Diary Notes:

Made in the USA
Lexington, KY
04 September 2019